A Bible Study for Girls, Grades 4-6

Beautiful In God's Eyes

Building Character, Wisdom, and Faith in Young Women

by Sharon Kennamer Bryant
and Dana Kennamer Hood

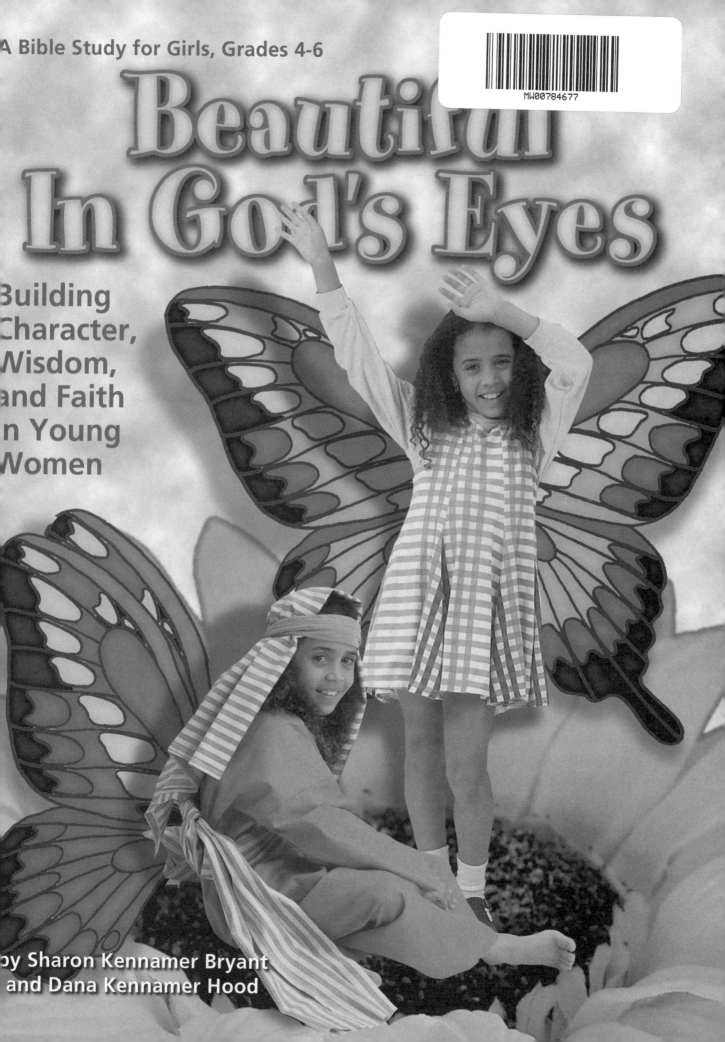

BEAUTIFUL IN GOD'S EYES

01 02 03 04 05 06 07 08 09 10—10 9 8 7 6 5 4 3 2 1
MANUFACTURED IN THE UNITED STATES OF AMERICA

Table of Contents

Introduction

Young people, especially girls, are bombarded daily with images of "beautiful people"; however, most of us cannot measure up to those images of perfection. These unrealistic attitudes lead to poor self-image, competition in clothing and makeup, and extreme cases of eating disorders and other obsessive behaviors. In this study you will be emphasizing that true beauty comes from the inside and is seen in our attitudes and behaviors. It does not come from what you look like on the outside. The class is designed for girls in grades four through six.

The study begins with a lesson that compares the world's standards of beauty with God's standards of beauty. The lessons that follow focus on eleven different women whose stories are found in the Bible. The lessons will emphasize a characteristic of each of these women that made them beautiful in God's eyes.

The last class meeting is designed to be a closing ceremony that is a graduation of sorts. It should be made very special for the girls. Tell them about it ahead of time and talk about it as the classes continue. Their parents or other caregivers and anyone else they would like to have present will be invited to share in the ceremony. There are suggestions for the ceremony in lesson thirteen. You can add or subtract what you like. Whatever you decide, try to make this as special and important to the girls as possible.

You might like to have a small gift to give to each girl to signify her completion of the course, as well as a certificate. A gift we have used is a small butterfly charm hung on a narrow ribbon for each girl to wear as a necklace. Oriental Trading Company Inc. has many small gifts that you can purchase. Their address is Omaha, NE 69103-2554. You can also find them online at www.oriental.com.

An important aspect of this experience is the commitment each girl makes to personal study and service during the week. Because of this, communication with the home is very important as you join in partnership with those who care for the girls to nurture their growing faith. Included with your course materials is a letter to be sent to the family of each girl in your class. It explains the purpose and goals of the class and communicates what the family can do to help. Be sure to send this to each family during the first week. Also, if you have new girls join the class as you go on be sure to send them a letter as well. You may choose to use this letter included in this resource, or to write your own, using the printed one as a guide.

You, as the teacher, are very important to the success of the class. The lessons provided are outlines with suggestions. Your own contributions will be what make the class valuable. Use these suggestions as you would like. Modify and add things that you find in your personal study. We encourage you to begin and to end each class with a prayer appropriate for the lesson. It will be a blessing for the girls as they hear you praying for them. This is also a good time for each girl to have the opportunity to pray for the things that concern her. During your personal devotional time each week, remember to lift up each of the girls individually to God in prayer. Our prayer is that as you share these ideas with the girls in your class, you too will be reminded of the beauty that God has placed inside you.

General Information

Reproducible Pages in This Booklet

1. Sample opening letter to families (see introduction).
2. Attendance chart — "Becoming Beautiful in God's Eyes."
3. Bible chart — "Let God's Word Change Your Life."
4. Memory work chart — "Write God's Word on Your Heart."
5. Heart cutout patterns — take-home memory work reminders.
6. Prayer partner reminder pattern.
7. Daily Bible reading chart — "Daily Beauty Treatment."
8. Personal spiritual discipline plan — "Spiritual Aerobics Training Plus."
9. Butterfly transfer for T-shirts.
10. Sample closing letter to families.
11. Completion certificate.
12. Closing ceremony invitation.

Lesson Components

Each lesson consists of the following components. In making your lesson plans, you will need to allow for each of these things.

1. Recording attendance.
2. Recording names of students who brought their Bibles.
3. Brief discussion of the daily beauty treatment for the past week.
4. Main story.
5. Activities, books.
6. Reciting of memory work.
7. Assignments for new memory work, readings, spiritual disciplines, and prayer partners for the following week.

Student Folders

Before the first class you should prepare a folder for each girl. Use a folder that has both paper fasteners and pockets to allow the girls to add things each week. Initially the folders should include one Bible chart, one memory work chart, twelve daily Bible reading charts, and one personal spiritual discipline plan. Each week the girls can place their memory work reminders, spiritual discipline commitments, and prayer partner names in the pockets. Decide ahead of time if you will decorate the fronts of the folders or use class time for the girls to decorate their own. When you have finished this course, you might like to bind each girl's folder with spiral bindings to make a more permanent book. Any business supply store can provide this service inexpensively. It is also possible that your education service center or local elementary school may have a binding machine that they would allow you to use if you provide the materials. The attendance chart would make a wonderful cover, if you do decide to bind the folders into booklets.

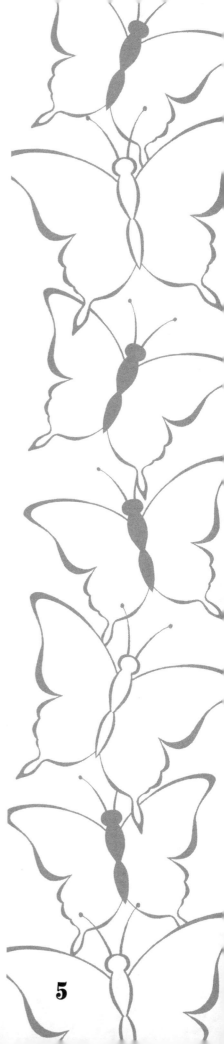

Books

Each lesson has a recommended book or books to read with the girls or to allow the girls to check out to read for themselves. Some of the books are religious publications; others are from secular literature. However, they have been selected because they illustrate the theme of the lesson. If your church library does not have these books, check your local public library. By planning ahead you can obtain most books through interlibrary loan service. It usually takes a week or two to receive a book in this way. Many of the books will also be available from your local elementary school library. You might also put a list of the books in your church newsletter or bulletin and ask that members who own the books loan them to you for the class. Be sure to send a thank-you note if you do obtain books in this way.

Attendance Charts

Communicate to the girls the importance of making a commitment to be present each week, not only to learn themselves, but also to encourage the other members of the class. The attendance chart included is a drawing of a mirror. To prepare these pages for use, you will need brightly colored photocopying paper, silver mylar sheets, craft "jewels" with one flat side, and jewelry adhesive. Mylar sheets can be found where wrapping paper is sold. They are generally displayed with tissue paper for placing in gift bags. The adhesive we use is E6000 Industrial Strength Adhesive and Sealant, which is available from MJDesigns, Ambers, Hobby Lobby, or other large craft houses. It is important that you use this type of adhesive because the charts will be laminated and other glues will not adhere to the surface. Photocopy one chart for each girl (and a few extra) on brightly colored paper. Cut out the mirror opening in each attendance chart. Cut a piece of mylar slightly larger than the opening and use a small amount of tape to attach it to another sheet of paper the same color as the chart. Make sure that the mylar is placed so that it will fill the cutout opening. Place the page with the mirror cutout over the mylar and tape it together at the top edge. Laminate each chart and use a permanent, fine-tip marker to write each girl's name on her chart. Each week that a girl is present, she will place a jewel on one of the spots indicated with dots to mark her attendance.

Bible Charts

One goal of this study is to impress upon the girls how important it is to be in God's Word. Encourage the girls to bring their Bibles each week. Be sure to use the Bibles in every class to reinforce the importance of bringing them. The chart for recording this is entitled, "Let God's Word Change Your Life." You will need multicolored round file stickers that can be placed over the small dots on the butterfly each week.

Important — Make sure that each girl has a Bible of her own to bring to class. If there is a girl who does not have a Bible, you can probably get one for her through the church or through an individual church member. Please do this discreetly so that the child is not embarrassed in front of the other girls. If several girls in the study do not have Bibles, the men's or women's groups in your church would probably be glad to provide them.

Memory Work Charts and Memory Reminder Cutouts

There will be a memory verse each week. This is called "Write God's Word on Your Heart." Write the Scripture on a poster or on the board. Read the verse aloud to the class. Then read it aloud in unison several times. Try covering phrases and learning the verse one portion at a time. Allow the girls to write the verse on their cutout hearts to take home with them as a reminder. They can put the heart someplace where they will see it every day. Be sure to take time to talk about the meaning of the verse. The next week allow each girl to recite the verse to you, and allow her to place a small heart sticker on her "Write God's Word on Your Heart" chart beside the appropriate verse. Do this during the time when the girls are working independently, instead of putting each girl on the spot in front of the others. Be sure to encourage girls to continue to work on verses they miss so that they can make these up in subsequent weeks.

Important — You may have students in your class who have learning disabilities. You might talk to the parents or to educators in your congregation for suggestions in dealing with these problems. Some options are to allow the girl to say the verse in her own words; give you the meaning of the verse; illustrate the verse; say only a part or the verse; or say the verse with you. Remember also that some children learn through hearing, and they may learn a verse better if someone will work orally with them. You might even make helping cassette recordings if you have children who are dyslexic. Remember to do this privately so that the girl is not embarrassed. Don't give up on these children memorizing — or at least learning about the verse. Sometimes it will just take them longer. Talk to the girls about what they would like to accomplish and help them set goals. Don't just assume that they cannot do the memory work.

Prayer Partners

An important part of spiritual formation is to develop a personal prayer life. Each week write the names of all the girls present in class on prayer partner reminders. Allow each girl to draw a name and to make a commitment to pray for her partner during the week. Include your name as well.

Bible Reading Chart

A chart entitled "Daily Beauty Treatment" is included to record the girls' daily Bible reading. One Scripture is assigned for each week. The girls will read that Scripture every day for that week. They may read it to themselves or to their parents, or have someone read it to them. There is a place at the top of the charts to record the reading for the week. The girls may ask their parents or caregivers to sign the chart on each day that they read. At the beginning of class each week, spend a little time talking about their reading from the previous week.

Spiritual Discipline Plan

Part of what the world considers physical beauty is a healthy, strong body. You get this by exercising. You can also do spiritual exercise. There are things we can do that are beautiful in God's eyes. If we practice doing these things instead of those that are against God's will, we will get stronger spiritually. Each time we do the right thing, it is easier to do the right thing the next time. (Just as the opposite is true — each time we do the wrong thing, it is easier to do the wrong thing the next time.) Each week the girls will choose a characteristic or behavior related to the week's lesson that is "Beautiful in God's Eyes." They will commit to practice this behavior during the week. Allow them to write their choices on their notebooks to remind themselves. Help them to be specific so that the behavior is easier to follow. For example, they might want to put, "Be kind." Instead, encourage them to choose something more specific, such as "not fight with my brother," or "share my toys with my sister." The goal of this exercise is to help the girls realize that the Bible and God are a part of our lives and should be used in dealing with day-to-day issues. We grow strong in God by doing what is right.

Important — With many of these areas, it would be helpful if you would participate as well. Be sure to learn the memory verse that is assigned. Read the daily Bible reading each day. Choose a behavior that you will practice during the week. And pray for each of the girls. This will not only serve as a good example for the girls, but it will also be a blessing for you as well.

T-shirts

A reproducible T-shirt transfer pattern is included in this book (page 63). Take the transfer pattern to a T-shirt company. They can produce an actual transfer from the pattern. They will also have a variety of lettering styles from which to choose. Encourage the girls to wear the shirts to class each week. This will be a way for them to feel that they are part of something special, and it will help them identify with the group. It is best if the girls are not asked to pay for these shirts, but that they are presented as a gift. We have found that placing a general announcement in the church bulletin explaining about the class and the shirts usually results in plenty of shirts. We include an estimated cost for the shirts in the announcement. We also spoke discreetly with parents who we knew could purchase their children's shirts and with other members who have been generous in the past with donations of this nature.

In lesson 11, we suggest that the girls decorate T-shirts for a younger class. You may want to determine how many shirts you will need for this activity and ask for donations for those shirts at the same time.

Letters to Families

On the next two pages you will find two letters to be sent to the families of each girl. The first of these would be sent during the first week of the class to gain the support of the family and to communicate with them the purpose of the study. The second letter should be sent during the tenth or eleventh week of the class. Its purpose is to ask family members to write a letter of blessing for their special girl to be read at the closing ceremony. The family blessing letters should be a surprise to the girls at the ceremony, so these should be sent through the mail or given to the parent personally. Be careful not to let the girls know these will be coming. You may use these letters just as they are. If you wish to write your own letter, there is a blank page (page 60) in the booklet that you may reproduce to use as your letterhead.

Important — These letters are written assuming that a parent is the primary caretaker for the child. We realize, however, that this is not always the case. If you have a child in your class who has a non-traditional family situation, you will want to revise the letter for her family.

Important — Be sure each child has a letter of blessing at the closing ceremony. If you do not get a response from the family, please make a phone call. Offer to help the family write the letter, or suggest that they might purchase an inspirational card to send. If you still do not have a letter for any girl, ask a member of the congregation to write one.

Note: The Scripture on the back can be printed as small or large as you like. It should probably take up less space on the shirt than shown.

Dear Parents,

I am so happy to have your daughter taking part in "Beautiful in God's Eyes." I look forward to spending this time teaching the girls, and I hope that the class will be a blessing for each of them.

This class will deal with the fact that beauty in God's eyes is not based on external appearance, but on the heart. Our attitudes and behaviors make us beautiful in God's eyes. Girls are constantly bombarded with images of physical perfection in our culture. This can lead to low self-image or competitive, judgmental behavior. I hope that in this class the girls can begin to see that they should judge themselves and others not by what is on the outside, but what comes from the inside.

The class is designed so that the girls will be doing work not only here, but also at home during the week as well. In this we will need your help. Each week your daughter will have a memory verse, a daily Bible reading, a prayer commitment, and a behavior to practice. Please help her work on learning her memory verse. She should read, or have read to her, the Bible reading selection each day. This is the same Scripture every day for a week. It would be helpful if you would discuss this Scripture with your daughter as well as reading it. She will have a chart that you can sign to help keep track of the readings. Each girl is also asked to make a commitment to pray for one classmate during the week. Encourage your daughter to be faithful to this commitment. Each week the girls will select something specific that they will work on in their own lives. Celebrate with your daughter's successes and support her when she struggles. Help her remember that God's grace covers us all as we seek to do God's will. The girls are encouraged to bring their Bibles each week. An occasional gentle reminder would be helpful.

I am excited about working with the girls during this time. I hope that if you have any questions or concerns, you will feel free to contact me. I hope also that you will pray for me as I take on the responsibility of teaching your daughter and the other girls.

Sincerely,

Dear Parents,

Your daughter will soon complete the study, "Beautiful in God's Eyes." On _____
we will be having a closing ceremony to affirm and honor the girls who participated in the class. We would like all the special people in the girls' families to attend this celebration. Please mark this date on your calendar and plan to attend.

As part of this ceremony, we would like to present each girl with letters of blessing from the people closest to her, especially from her parents. These letters should be positive and supportive, expressing love and pride for her, thankfulness to God for the blessing she brings, and hopes and prayers for her future. Please bring any letters of blessing with you to the ceremony. If you will be unable to attend, you may send your letter to me at the address below. Make sure that you send your letter in plenty of time to arrive before the ceremony.

If you have any questions, please feel free to call me at _____. Thank you for sharing your precious girl with me over these past few weeks. It has been a blessing to watch her grow in the Lord.

Sincerely,

Name

Address

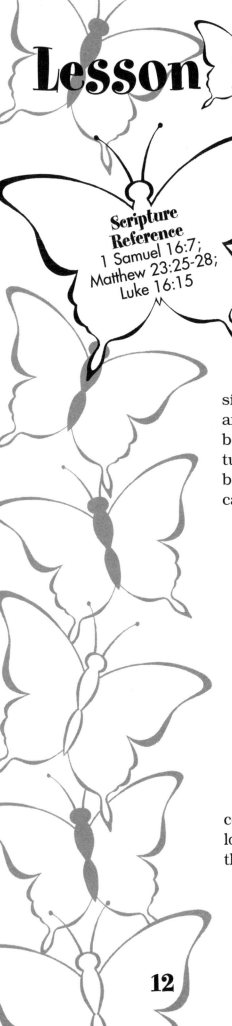

Lesson 1 Looking on the Heart

Scripture Reference
1 Samuel 16:7;
Matthew 23:25-28;
Luke 16:15

The purpose of this first lesson is to introduce the focus of the study to the girls. Explain to them that the lessons you will be studying are about women in the Bible who were pleasing to God. The Bible doesn't tell us what these women looked like — whether they were short, tall, thin, or chubby. Instead the Bible tells us what they did and how they treated others.

Bring pictures from magazines that show what society considers "beautiful" people. People Magazine annually publishes an edition naming the fifty most beautiful people. This would be a good source for you, if you can locate it. Look at the pictures and talk about the things that we often use to judge beauty (body shape, hair color and style, facial features, physical fitness, clothing, and so forth).

Ask: Do most people look like the people in the magazine?

Say: No, most of us look very ordinary. But still we judge others by the unrealistic standards set by the magazines, movies, and television. We often do not feel good about ourselves because we do not look like the models in the magazines. And sometimes we make fun of others who are not beautiful by the world's standards. But the things that people use to judge beauty are not the same as what God uses. What we look like on the outside or what we wear is not really important. What is important is what is on the inside.

Read the Scriptures with the girls and talk about what God considers beautiful. God does not look at the outside. God looks at the inside, at our hearts. God looks at the way we think and the way we behave.

Activity Choices

1. Before class cut large hearts from red construction paper. Using an instant-developing camera, take a picture of each of the girls. Allow each girl to glue her picture in the middle of a heart. Suggest that the girls write around their pictures some attitudes and behaviors that make us beautiful to God. Talk about these things as the girls work. Give the girls a contrasting piece of construction paper on which to write the title, "Beautiful in God's Eyes." After the girls glue their hearts to this piece of paper, the project can be placed in their folders. You might want to display the hearts on the wall for several weeks before putting them in the folders.

2. To prepare for this activity you will need to cut out small red hearts for the girls to write on. Each girl will need a number of hearts equal to the number of girls in the class. Allow each girl to share something about herself with the class —something that she does well or something of which she is proud. Then allow the other girls to write a positive comment about her on a heart and give these to her.

Activity Supplies
1. construction paper, scissors, instant-developing camera, glue, pens or pencils
2. red construction paper, scissors, pens or pencils

Suggested Books

The Paper Bag Princess by Robert N. Munsch. This is the story of a princess who, through her wit and intelligence, rescues a handsome, well-dressed prince from a dragon. However, all of her clothing has been burned by the dragon's fires, so all she has left to wear is a paper bag. When he is rescued by the princess, all the prince can see is that she is wearing a paper bag. He cannot see her value as a person. She realizes that while he looks like a prince on the outside, on the inside he is not someone she wants to know.

Big Al by Andrew Clements. Big Al is an ugly fish who frightens all the other fish with his looks. However, when they are captured by the fisherman's net, Big Al rescues them. The other fish learn to look at Big Al in a different way and become his friend.

Write God's Word on Your Heart

Proverbs 31:30

Daily Beauty Treatment

Matthew 6:25-34. This Scripture talks about how important each of us is to God. Remind the girls to read this Scripture every day this week and to have their parents sign their charts.

Write God's
Word on
Your Heart
Proverbs 31:30

Daily Beauty
Treatment
Matthew 6:25-34

Spiritual Aerobics

Encourage the girls to choose a behavior that they will try to practice this week. Have them write these down in their folders to take home with them.

Moses' Mother
Love and Unselfishness

Lesson 2

Scripture Reference
Exodus 1:1–2:10

We all know stories of Moses. He was a great leader of God's people. But when he was born, things were very different. Moses' mother and father were Israelites who lived in Egypt. Many years before the Israelites had come to Egypt as honored guests, but now they were slaves. They were forced to work very hard for Pharaoh, the king of Egypt. Pharaoh did not trust the Israelites. There were many of them, and Pharaoh was afraid they would try to take over his country. For this reason Pharaoh made a very cruel law. He ordered that all baby boys of the Israelites be thrown into the river to die. In this way there would not be so many new Israelites growing up to take over his country. Even though Pharaoh made this law, the midwives, who were women who helped the babies be born, did not always obey. They secretly let many of the baby boys live.

It was at this time that Moses was born. His mother was very frightened for him and hid him as best she could for three months. But when he was that old, it became very difficult for her to continue to hide him. She did not want her son to be killed, so she made a plan. She took a basket and covered it with tar and pitch to make it waterproof. Then she carefully put Moses in the basket and hid it among the reeds at the edge of the river. Moses' mother asked his sister, Miriam, to hide near the basket to watch what happened to Moses.

Soon Miriam saw some women coming to the river. One of the women was Pharaoh's daughter, a princess of Egypt. She was coming to the river with her servants to bathe. As she got to the river, she saw the basket and sent one of the slave girls to get it. She opened the basket and saw baby Moses. He was crying, and she felt sorry for him. She knew that he was one of the Hebrew babies, but she did not want him to die. She decided to take him as her own son.

When Miriam saw this, she rushed over to talk to the princess. "Would you like me to find one of the Hebrew women to nurse this baby for you?" Miriam asked. The princess agreed, and Miriam went to get her mother. The princess told

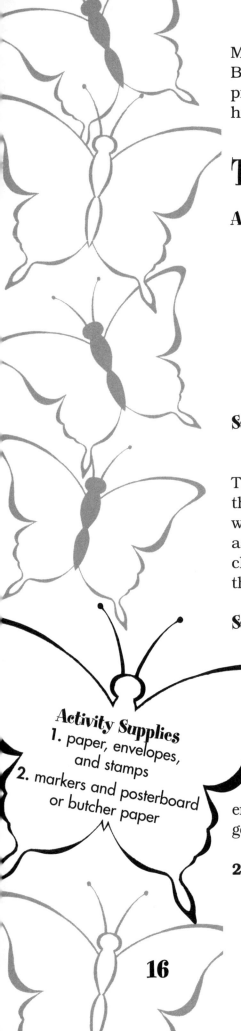

Moses' mother that she would be paid to take care of Moses. But when he was old enough, Moses would become the princess' adopted son. Moses' mother was able to take care of him for a while, but to save his life she had to give him up.

To Talk About

Ask: Do you think that Moses' mother loved him?

How do you think she felt when she had to give him up to the princess?

Do you think she wanted to give up her son?

Why did she do this? (*Her actions showed great love and unselfishness. She did not do what she really wanted, because it would not be best for Moses. She had to give him up to save his life.*)

Say: Love is not selfish. When we love someone, sometimes we have to be unselfish.

Talk about times that the girls have been unselfish with those they love. Talk about times the girls' parents or someone else who loves them has been unselfish toward them. (For example, ask about times their parents or someone else did what the children wanted instead of what they wanted, or about times their parents or someone else gave up something for them.)

Say: God tells us to love one another. We can see from this example that part of that loving is being unselfish. What are ways that we can be unselfish to those around us?

Activity Supplies
1. paper, envelopes, and stamps
2. markers and posterboard or butcher paper

Activity Choices

1. Have the girls write a thank-you note to someone thanking that person for his or her unselfishness. Provide paper, envelopes, and stamps for the letters. When the girls are finished, go to the mailbox as a group and put the letters in to be mailed.

2. Divide the girls into groups of two to four. Provide each group with markers and posterboard or butcher paper. Have them think of unselfish things that people have done for them or ways that they themselves can be unselfish. Give them several minutes to work on this; then discuss these things together with the entire class.

16

Suggested Books

The Giving Tree by Shel Silverstein. In this classic book a tree gives all she has to make a boy happy.

A Chair for My Mother by Vera B. Williams. A family who loses everything in a fire works together to save enough money for a new chair for their mother. They also experience the love of others around them who give furniture and other items to replace those lost in the fire.

Rainbow Fish by Marcus Pfister. A beautiful fish with shiny scales discovers that true joy comes from giving.

Write God's Word on Your Heart

Ephesians 5:21. Talk about what it means to submit to one another or to be subject to one another. This means to consider what is best for the other person — not always just what you want to do, but being unselfish in love for another person because of Jesus and what he has done for us. Jesus was unselfish in a way none of us can match by giving his life to save all of us.

Write God's
Word on
Your Heart
Ephesians 5:21

Daily Beauty Treatment

1 Corinthians 13. This is the well-known chapter about love. Ask the girls as they read this week to see what things they can learn about love and what God wants from us from this chapter.

Daily Beauty
Treatment
1 Corinthians 13

Spiritual Aerobics

Encourage each girl to think of some way she can be unselfish this week. Again encourage them to be specific, instead of just saying, "I will be unselfish." Have them think of ways they may have trouble being unselfish and work on this during the week. If you have time, you might talk a little about successes or difficulties with last week's aerobics.

Lesson 3 Rahab
Courage

Scripture Reference
Joshua 2; 6:22-23

In this story you will learn about a woman of great courage. Her name was Rahab. When God brought the people of Israel out of slavery in Egypt, God led them to the Promised Land. However, at first the people did not have enough faith to believe that God would help them take the land. Because the people did not have faith, God let them wander in the wilderness for forty years. Finally the forty years were over. The people had a new leader. His name was Joshua. They were once again camped by the Jordan River waiting to go into the land that God had promised to them. Joshua sent two men into the land to find out what they could about the city of Jericho. This was the first city that they planned to take.

While the spies were in Jericho, a woman named Rahab allowed them to stay in her home. Someone saw these men and went to the king to tell him, "Look! Some of the Israelites have come here to spy on us." So the king sent a message to Rahab. He told her to bring out the men who were staying in her house. But Rahab did not do as the king asked. Instead, she took the two men up on her roof and hid them under bundles of flax, a plant that she used to make cloth. This took great courage, because she would have been in trouble if the men had been found in her home after she had refused to send them out to the king. When the messengers came to her door and told her to bring the men out, she said, "They were here, but they left. If you go quickly, you may catch up with them." So the men went looking for the spies somewhere else.

Then Rahab went up to the roof to talk to the spies. She said, "I know that the Lord has given you this land. All of the people who live here are afraid because they have heard about the things your God has done for you. Now, promise me that you will show kindness to me and my family because I have taken care of you. Give me a sign that my family and I will be saved when you take the city of Jericho."

The men promised Rahab that they would save her life and the lives of her family, just as she had saved the lives of the spies. They gave her a scarlet (explain that a scarlet is a bright

18

red color) cord to hang out her window when the Israelites attacked. They said, "Gather your family here and keep them inside. Hang this scarlet cord out your window, and you will all be safe."

In those days cities were surrounded by high walls. Some houses were built into the walls. Rahab's house was in the wall of the city. Her window looked outside the wall. She let a rope down out of her window and lowered the men to the ground. They left her house and hid in the hills for three days until the men stopped looking for them; then they returned to Joshua with the things that they had learned about Jericho.

Later, when the Israelites took the city of Jericho, something amazing happened. Remember that the walls of the city fell when the Israelites walked around them? But the house of Rahab, which was in the wall, was not destroyed. Just as the men had promised, Rahab and all of her family were saved. Later, Rahab is mentioned in Matthew 1:5 as one of the ancestors of Jesus. She was saved because of her faith and courage.

To Talk About

Ask: What is courage? Does it just mean not being afraid? (*Allow answers.*)

Say: Courage is more than not being afraid. Courage means doing the right thing even if you are afraid or even when it is difficult.

Ask: How did Rahab show courage? (*by defying the king and hiding the spies*) What do you think would have happened to her if the men had been found hidden in her home?

Say: We are not threatened physically because of our faith, but sometimes we may be uncomfortable talking about our beliefs.

Ask: What are some of those times? (*Allow answers.*) What are some ways we can show courage in following God?

Activity Choices

1. Using red embroidery floss or red cord, allow the girls to make bracelets by knotting or braiding the floss or cord. The bracelets will serve as a reminder of how God kept God's promise to Rahab when she hung the red cord from her window. Talk about how the bracelets can also be a reminder that God keeps God's promises to us and that we should have courage in doing God's will in our lives.

2. Encourage the girls to make an acrostic using the word *courage*. An acrostic is a simple poem in which a word is written vertically, and each letter is used to begin a line of the poem consisting of a word or phrase. The words and phrases should describe or explain some aspect of the base word. See the example:

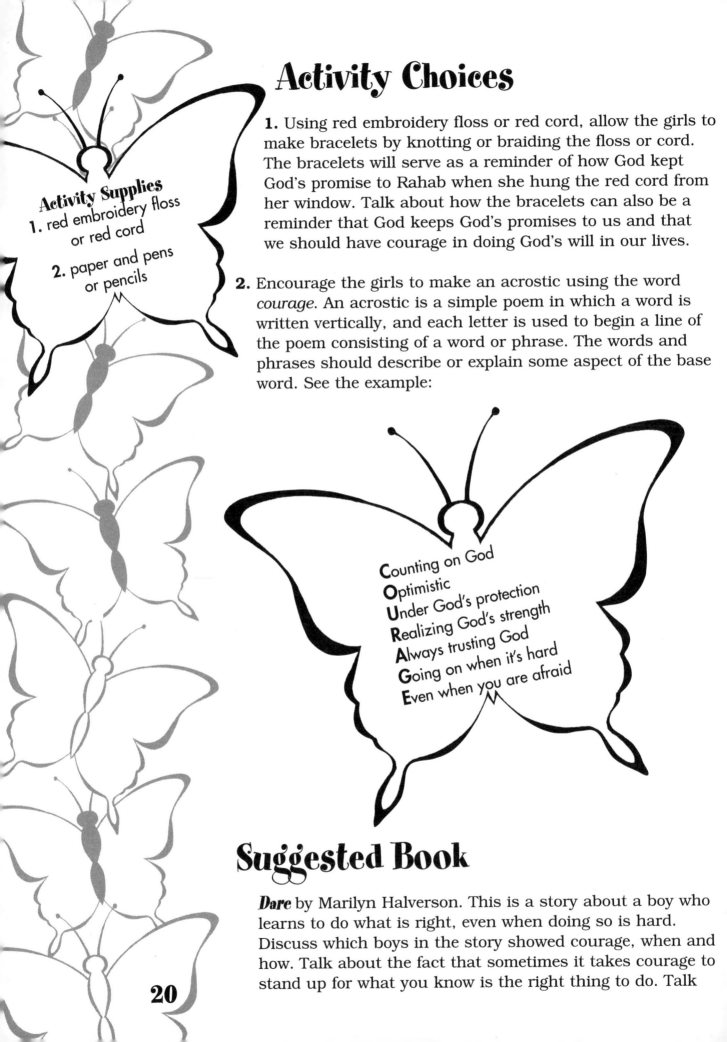

Activity Supplies
1. red embroidery floss or red cord
2. paper and pens or pencils

Counting on God
Optimistic
Under God's protection
Realizing God's strength
Always trusting God
Going on when it's hard
Even when you are afraid

Suggested Book

Dare by Marilyn Halverson. This is a story about a boy who learns to do what is right, even when doing so is hard. Discuss which boys in the story showed courage, when and how. Talk about the fact that sometimes it takes courage to stand up for what you know is the right thing to do. Talk about things that the girls encounter that make it hard to do the right things—cheating, lying, bad words, disobeying, and so forth.

Write God's Word on Your Heart

Hebrews 13:6

Daily Beauty Treatment

Psalm 23. This psalm is a reminder that God takes care of us. Even when things are not going well, God is with us.

Spiritual Aerobics

Help the girls think of a situation that they encounter each week in which it is difficult for them to do the right thing. Encourage them to make a commitment to do the right thing in this situation this week.

Lesson 4 Deborah
Leadership

Scripture Reference
Judges 4–5

When the Israelites first lived in the land of Canaan, the land that had been promised to them, they did not have a king. It was a time when the Israelites sometimes forgot God because the people who lived around them worshiped idols. When the people of God began to worship idols and forgot about what God had done for them, God would allow one of the nations around them to conquer the people of Israel. Finally, they would remember God and pray to God for deliverance. God was very patient with the people. God would send a leader to help them overcome those who had conquered them.

One of the leaders was a woman named Deborah. During the time of Deborah, the Canaanites had conquered Israel. For twenty years the Canaanite leader, Sisera, had led his powerful armies in controlling Israel. Sisera had nine hundred iron chariots that his army used in battle. Finally the Israelites cried out to God for help. Deborah was a judge and a very wise woman. She would sit under a palm tree between Ramah and Bethel, and the people would come to her for help in settling their problems with one another.

One day Deborah sent for a man named Barak. God had given Deborah a message for Barak. God wanted Barak to take an army of ten thousand men to attack the army of Sisera. God promised to help Barak defeat the Canaanite army. But Barak said to Deborah, "I will go only if you will go with me." Deborah agreed to go with Barak, but because of his lack of faith, he would not receive the glory of the battle — a woman would.

So Barak went to attack the armies of Sisera. When Barak led the attack, God delivered the Canaanites over to the Israelite army.

All of the Israelites celebrated this great victory. They sang songs honoring Deborah and Barak and thanking God for giving them the victory. After this victory the Israelites lived in peace and followed God for forty years.

To Talk About

Say: Deborah was respected for her wisdom, and the people looked to her as a leader.

Deborah listened to what God said.

Deborah led quietly by obeying God and helping people with their problems.

Through God's power the Israelite army defeated the more powerful Canaanite army.

Ask: How can we be leaders? We can be examples by obeying God. We can stand up for what is right, even when others want to do the wrong thing. We can be helpful and kind to those around us. We can listen to what God says.

Important: Girls may have questions about the use of violence in solving problems. Explain that during the time of the Israelites, it was common for nations to make war against one another and that sometimes there was no other way of defeating the enemy except through the death of the enemy. God calls us to peace, not to violence. Today we strive to find other ways of dealing with conflict. Reassure the girls that no matter what happens, God does not forget God's people. If any of the girls tells you that violence has been used against her, remember that it is your legal duty to report what you have heard.

Activity Choices

Activity Supplies
1. posterboard, marker, paper, pens or pencils

1. Talk about good leaders and bad leaders. Sometimes people are leaders by being bullies. Sometimes people lead others to do bad things. This is not the kind of leadership God talks about. Divide a piece of posterboard into two columns. Mark one column "Good Leaders," and the other "Bad Leaders." Give each girl a sheet of paper and have her mark the paper to match the poster. Talk about characteristics of good and bad leaders and list those characteristics on the poster. The girls should copy the lists onto their papers to save in their folders.

A good discussion point would be to think of good and bad leaders in the Bible. Other examples to look at are leaders from history, such as Abraham Lincoln and Adolph Hitler.

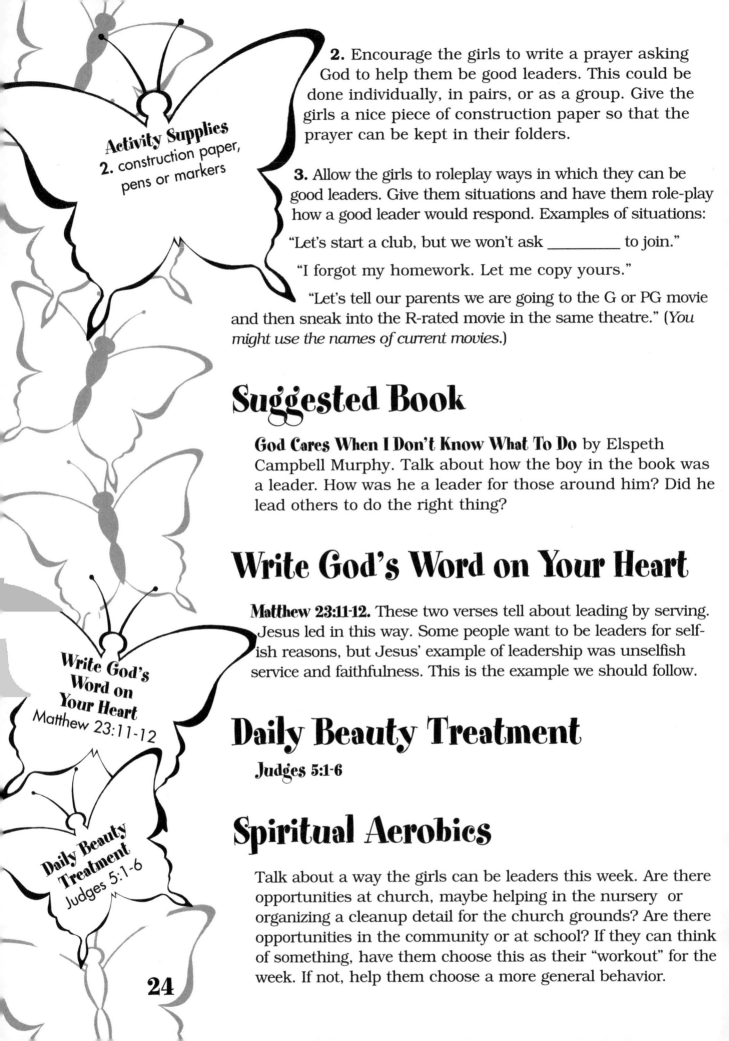

2. Encourage the girls to write a prayer asking God to help them be good leaders. This could be done individually, in pairs, or as a group. Give the girls a nice piece of construction paper so that the prayer can be kept in their folders.

3. Allow the girls to roleplay ways in which they can be good leaders. Give them situations and have them role-play how a good leader would respond. Examples of situations:

"Let's start a club, but we won't ask _____ to join."

"I forgot my homework. Let me copy yours."

"Let's tell our parents we are going to the G or PG movie and then sneak into the R-rated movie in the same theatre." (*You might use the names of current movies.*)

Activity Supplies
2. construction paper, pens or markers

Suggested Book

God Cares When I Don't Know What To Do by Elspeth Campbell Murphy. Talk about how the boy in the book was a leader. How was he a leader for those around him? Did he lead others to do the right thing?

Write God's Word on Your Heart

Matthew 23:11-12. These two verses tell about leading by serving. Jesus led in this way. Some people want to be leaders for selfish reasons, but Jesus' example of leadership was unselfish service and faithfulness. This is the example we should follow.

Write God's Word on Your Heart
Matthew 23:11-12

Daily Beauty Treatment

Judges 5:1-6

Daily Beauty Treatment
Judges 5:1-6

Spiritual Aerobics

Talk about a way the girls can be leaders this week. Are there opportunities at church, maybe helping in the nursery or organizing a cleanup detail for the church grounds? Are there opportunities in the community or at school? If they can think of something, have them choose this as their "workout" for the week. If not, help them choose a more general behavior.

Ruth
Loyalty

Scripture Reference The Book of Ruth

Lesson 5

Naomi and Elimelech were Israelites who lived in Bethlehem. They married and had two sons named Mahlon and Chilion. There was a famine in the land of Israel. This means that there was no rain and no crops would grow. There was not enough food for the people who lived there. Naomi and Elimelech decided that they would take their family and move to a country where they could find food. They moved to the country of Moab and lived there for many years.

The boys grew up and fell in love and married young women from the land of Moab. One married a young woman named Orpah, and the other married a young woman named Ruth. But after a while a very sad thing happened. Naomi's husband, Elimelech, died, and so did both of her sons. Naomi was very lonely being so far away from her homeland and her relatives. She heard that the famine in Israel was over, so she decided to go home. Both Orpah and Ruth started the journey back to Israel with Naomi, but Naomi realized that they might be better off if they returned to the homes they had grown up in. She told the two young women to return to their families.

Orpah agreed to go home to her family. She hugged Naomi and said goodbye. But Ruth refused to go. She loved her mother-in-law very much. "Where you go, I will go," Ruth said. "Your people will be my people, and your God will be my God." Naomi was very happy to have Ruth with her. When they reached Bethlehem, Naomi's old friends welcomed her back.

It was time for the barley harvest. Because Naomi and Ruth did not have husbands, they needed to find a way to get food and money. It was the custom of that time for the harvesters to leave the grain that they dropped for the needy people to pick up. Ruth went to the fields to pick up (glean) this grain so that she could bring it home for herself and Naomi. Ruth showed her loyalty to Naomi again by working hard to get food for them. The field that she worked in happened to belong to a man named Boaz, who was a relative of Elimelech.

Boaz saw Ruth and asked his workers about her. He told them to be kind to her and to let extra grain fall so that she

could pick it up. He also allowed her to drink from the water that was intended for his workers. Boaz asked Ruth to sit with him at lunchtime and to share his food. He told her that she should work only in his fields and not go to any other fields. Ruth worked in the fields belonging to Boaz for the entire harvest time. During that time Boaz came to love Ruth.

Boaz asked Ruth to marry him. She was very happy, and they were married. After a while they had a baby boy whom they named Obed. Ruth and Boaz were very happy. Naomi was very happy too. Ruth was like a daughter to her, and Obed was like the grandson that she had never had. Naomi was happy to help Boaz and Ruth take care of their son. They were thankful that God had taken care of them and had given them a new family.

To Talk About

Ask: What does it mean to be loyal?

How did Ruth show loyalty?

Why do you think that Ruth went with Naomi? How did Ruth feel about Naomi?

How can we show loyalty? (*Remind the girls that our first loyalty should be to God. If being loyal to those around us would make us disobey God, we should not do it. You might help them think of an example, such as a friend who is doing something wrong and wants you to help, or a friend who is doing something that will harm her and asks you not to tell.*)

What are some examples of loyalty to friends, family, and so forth? What are some examples of disloyalty?

Can we say that God is loyal? (*God is the ultimate example of loyalty. Talk about ways that God and Jesus show loyalty.*)

Activity Supplies
1. copy of the acrostic, pencils
2. cookie cutters or sponges, pieces of construction paper, and a couple of colors of paint
3. construction paper, markers or crayons, envelopes, stamps

Activity Choices

1. Let the girls write an acrostic using the word *loyal* or *loyalty* as the base. See the directions for writing an acrostic in Lesson 3. You might write one acrostic as a group on the board or let the girls work individually or in pairs. Make sure each girl has a copy of the acrostic to place in her folder.

2. Find cookie cutters or sponges in the shape of children. Give the girls several pieces of construction paper and a couple of colors of paint. Allow the girls to print shapes using the cookie cutters or sponges to represent their friends. Encourage them to write the names of their friends and something about each one for which they thank God. As the girls work, talk about ways that we show loyalty to our friends. When the pages are dry, the girls can add them to their folders.

3. Encourage each girl to design a thank-you card for someone who has shown loyalty to her. If possible, arrange to mail the cards.

Suggested Book

Rosie and Michael by Judith Viorst. Rosie and Michael both pledge to remain loyal to each other, even if the rest of the world has turned against them. Talk about loyal friends and what a gift they are from God. You might let each girl share a time when one of her friends was loyal.

Write God's Word on Your Heart

Ruth 1:16. Verse 17 continues the thought, and you might read it with the girls, but verse 16 gets the thought across.

Daily Beauty Treatment

Psalm 136. This reading tells us how God is loyal. Look at it briefly with the girls and note the repetition of the phrase, "His love endures forever." This is an indication of God's faithfulness and loyalty. We can always count on God.

Spiritual Aerobics

Be sure to have the girls choose a behavior they will try to practice this week.

Lesson 6 Hannah
Prayer and Faithfulness

Scripture Reference
1 Samuel 1:1–2:11

There was a man named Elkanah who had a wife named Hannah, whom he loved very much. They were Jews. Hannah wanted children, but had none. This made her very sad.

Each year Elkanah and Hannah went to Shiloh, where they visited the tabernacle to worship God. One day while they were at Shiloh, Hannah grew very sad thinking about not having a child. She began to cry. When Elkanah found her crying, he tried to comfort her by reminding her of his love for her. But Hannah could not be comforted. She was so sad, she could not even eat.

After the dinner hour Hannah went to the tabernacle to pray to God. She told God how sad she was that she did not have any children. She was crying as she prayed. Hannah asked God to send her a baby boy, and she made a promise — if God would send her a son, she would dedicate her son to God, and her son would serve God all his life.

Eli, the priest, was in the tabernacle. Hannah did not see him while she was praying. Eli could see Hannah's lips moving as she prayed, but he could not hear her. He knew something was wrong with Hannah. Eli spoke to Hannah and asked her what was wrong. She explained why she had been praying. Eli saw that Hannah was a faithful woman and told her not to be sad. He said, "God will answer your prayer."

When Hannah left the tabernacle, she felt much better. She went back to her tent and ate. She was happy that she had talked to God, and she believed that God would answer her prayer.

The next morning Elkanah and Hannah left to return home. Before they started their journey, they worshiped God and prayed, just as we often pray to God to keep us safe as we leave for a trip.

God remembered Hannah and answered her prayer. Hannah gave birth to a baby boy, whom she named Samuel. This name means "asked of God." Hannah was very happy. She took good care of her son. When Elkanah went back to Shiloh to worship the next year, Hannah did not go with him. She said, "I will stay home until Samuel is old enough to stay at the tabernacle. Then he will live there with Eli and help him. Samuel will be God's servant. God gave Samuel to me, and I promised to give him back to God."

Samuel grew, and Hannah took care of him. His parents loved him very much. Soon Samuel was old enough to stay in the temple. That year Hannah and Samuel went with Elkanah to Shiloh. When they arrived, Hannah took Samuel to Eli. She reminded Eli whom she was and explained that Samuel was the son whom God had given her in answer to her prayer. Hannah explained to Eli that she had promised that Samuel would be God's servant.

Samuel stayed with Eli. Part of Eli's job was taking care of the tabernacle. Samuel helped him do this. Eli was glad to have Samuel there to help him. Samuel wore a small coat like the one Eli had.

Every year Samuel's mother and father made the trip to Shiloh to worship God. Hannah made a new coat for Samuel each year and brought it to him. Eli blessed Elkanah and Hannah for what they had done. He said, "May the Lord give you many children for the one you have given to serve him." God heard Eli's blessing and gave Hannah three more sons and two daughters. Hannah was faithful to her promise to God, even though it was difficult. Because of this, God blessed her with more children.

To Talk About

Say: Hannah made a promise, and she kept it.

Ask: Was it an easy promise to keep? Do you think she ever wished she could keep Samuel at home?

Do you think God keeps God's promises? (*Think of some examples with the girls of times that God kept a promise.*)

Is it important that we keep the promises we make?

Say: If it is important to keep promises, we should be very careful in the promises we make.

Hannah prayed to God about her problem. God answered her prayer. God answers our prayers also. We can talk to God about our problems.

Activity Choices

Activity Supplies
1. posterboard, marker, paper, pens or pencils
2. hymnal, Bible, paper, pens or pencils

1. Talk about the different types of prayers we can pray. Sometimes we think praying is something we only do at certain times or that we only do at church. But that is not true. We can pray anywhere. We can pray at any time. We can also pray about many different kinds of things. God will always listen to us. We pray to God for many different reasons. We say prayers of praise for the wonders of creation. We pray in thanksgiving for the ways God has worked in our lives. Sometimes we pray to God for ourselves or for others when we are struggling with sin or sadness or when our bodies need healing from sickness. We also ask God for forgiveness.

Begin a prayer list with your class. Prepare a poster with four columns labeled "Praise," "Thanksgiving," "Supplication," and "Confession." Make sure the girls understand each category. (We praise God for what God has done; we express our gratitude for God's gifts to us; we tell God about something we have done wrong or have not done and say we are sorry; we ask for God's help.)

Together think of several prayers to put under each category. Remember to be specific. Invite the girls to make their own four-column prayer list for their folders. Spend some time in prayer with your class about the things on your list. This might be a good thing to continue and to build on each week. Model the importance of prayer by praying in each class. Send a note to a different girl each week, saying, "I remembered you and thanked God for you in prayer today."

2. Letters to God. We think of prayer as a time when we sit and talk to God, but prayer can take many forms. It can be a song, a poem, or a letter. Look in the hymnal for hymns that are actually prayers. Look at the Book of Psalms for examples of poetic prayers, and look at Paul's letters for other prayers. Invite the girls to write a letter to God. Before they start, encourage them to think about what they want to say. Also remind them of the different things they can include in this letter (praise, thanksgiving, supplication, confession). Write your own letter to God. When the girls have finished, let them put their letters in their folders.

Suggested Books

What Can I Say to You, God? or **God Cares When I Need to Talk To Somebody**, both by Elspeth Campbell Murphy. Either of these is a good discussion starter for a talk about prayer. If it is possible to give the girls individual prayer journals, **Hey, God! Let's Talk** combines explanations of the types of prayer, examples of prayers, Bible prayers, and room for writing your own prayers.

Here are some good "talk points" to use with any of these books:

God answers prayers.
We should pray specifically.
We can pray to God about anything, not just "the big things."
We should have a special time of prayer with God every day.
God listens to everyone, even children. We cannot understand how, but God is able to do this.
We do not have to use special big words when we talk to God. We can talk to him just like we would to anyone else.
Our prayers should not be focused entirely on asking for things. Other things we should include in our prayers are praise, thanksgiving, confession, and prayers for others.

Write God's Word on Your Heart

1 Samuel 1:27

Daily Beauty Treatment

James 5:13-18

Spiritual Aerobics

Since the lesson today is about prayer, the girls might make a commitment to pray every day this week. Encourage them to be specific in their goal. For example, encourage them to say, "I will pray before I go to bed each night," rather than, "I will pray every day." This will help them focus on their goal.

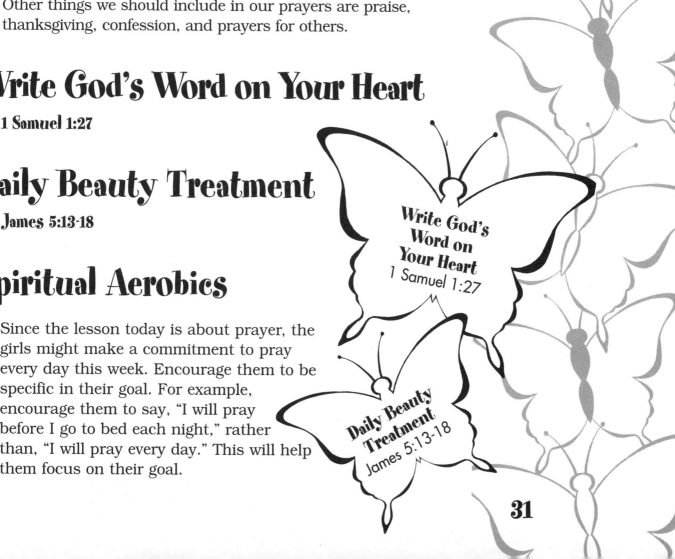

Write God's Word on Your Heart
1 Samuel 1:27

Daily Beauty Treatment
James 5:13-18

31

Lesson 7 Elizabeth
Rejoicing

Scripture Reference
Luke 1:5-25, 39-45, 57-80

Around the time that Jesus was born in Bethlehem, a priest, Zechariah, and his wife, Elizabeth, lived in a little town in the hill country of Judea. Zechariah was descended from the priestly group of Abijah, and Elizabeth was from the family of Aaron, Moses' brother. This couple was righteous and followed God's laws. However, they did not have children, and they were growing old.

One time when it was Zechariah's turn to serve as a priest, he was inside offering incense, and an angel appeared to him. "Do not be afraid," the angel said. "Your wife will give birth to a son. You must name him John. He will become a very special man and will lead many of the people of Israel back to their God." Zechariah did not believe the angel; after all, he and Elizabeth were growing old. "Because you did not believe me, you will not be able to speak until all that I have told you happens," the angel said.

Zechariah went home. He could not speak. He could only write notes to Elizabeth. Soon they discovered that Elizabeth was going to have a baby, just as the angel had said. Elizabeth was delighted about what God had done for her.

As Elizabeth waited for her baby to be born, an angel made a visit to Nazareth. Mary, a young cousin of Elizabeth, lived there. The angel told Mary that she too would have a baby, but this baby would be the Son of God. Mary rushed to the village where Elizabeth lived to talk to her about this very special baby. Elizabeth was overjoyed about Mary's news. She rejoiced that she was able to know the mother of the promised Messiah.

When Elizabeth's baby was born, all of her family came to rejoice with her. On the eighth day, when it was time to name him as was the custom, the family members wanted to name the baby after Zechariah. "No, no," Elizabeth said. "His name is John." The family members were amazed, because there was no one in their family named John, and it was the tradition to name a boy child after his father or some other male relative. They turned to Zechariah. He was still unable to speak, and he wrote on a tablet, "His name is John." When he had written this, suddenly he was able to speak again and began praising God. All the people were amazed by this and wondered about this special child who had been born.

To Talk About

Ask: What things did Elizabeth rejoice about? (*She rejoiced abut her own baby, but she also rejoiced that the baby Mary was expecting would become our Savior.*)

Say: There are many things that we have to rejoice about. We have been given many gifts. We also can rejoice that Jesus came to this world and lived to give us an example and died to save us.

Activity Choices

1. Mix water, tempera paint, and a small amount of liquid dish detergent. Use a good bit of tempera paint to get a good, strong color. Provide several colors in small bowls. You will also need straws. Provide each girl with a piece of construction paper and a straw. Ask them to write the Bible verse, "Rejoice in the Lord always; again I will say again, Rejoice" (Philippians 4:4), across the top of their paper. Then allow them to make bubble prints by blowing gently in the paint/detergent solution until the bubbles rise over the top of the bowl. Turn the paper upside down on top of the bubbles, lifting a print onto the paper. The prints will be light in color. As the girls work, talk about how praise and rejoicing bubbles up inside of us when we realize the things that God and Jesus have done for us. You might like to sing some songs of rejoicing with the girls as they work.

2. In many cases in the Bible, when someone wants to rejoice about something that God has done, that person invites his or her friends to a feast to help celebrate. Remember the prodigal son and the story of the lost coin. Have a "Rejoice Party" to celebrate all the things that God has done for you. Buy a cake (or bake one yourself) with "God loves us!" or some other appropriate caption written in frosting on the top. As you celebrate, talk about the blessings God has given. Try to encourage the girls to think of some blessings that are not connected to material good.

Activity Supplies
1. water, tempera paint, liquid dish detergent, small bowls, drinking straws, paper, pens
2. cake, frosting, paper plates, napkins, forks

33

Suggested Book

Everybody Shout Hallelujah! by Elspeth Campbell Murphy. Talk about all the things we have to rejoice about. If you are planning to do the bubble prints, there is a section in this book that talks about bubbles in reference to praise.

Write God's Word on Your Heart

Philippians 4:4

Daily Beauty Treatment

Luke 1:57-66

Spiritual Aerobics

Encourage the girls in some praise-oriented goal. For example, they might commit to think of two or three things at the end of each day for which they can rejoice and praise God. Have them record their thoughts on a sheet of paper labeled "My Week of Praise." At the end of each day they can pray to God with praise and thanksgiving for these things. This paper can be put in their folders at the end of the week. This could also be an exercise that you could encourage them to continue even after the week is over. Be on the lookout for inexpensive journals or diaries. By the middle of the year they are often marked down to almost nothing. If you do find some, get them for the girls to encourage recording praise and prayers.

Write God's
Word on
Your Heart
Philippians 4:4

Daily Beauty
Treatment
Luke 1:57-66

Mary, the Mother of Jesus
Chosen by God

Scripture Reference
Luke 1:26-38, 46-49

This lesson is not about the birth of Jesus; it is about the choosing of Mary as his mother.

In the first lesson of this study we talked about how God does not look on the outside of people, but on the inside. When God chose David as the new king instead of his older brothers, God was seeing what David could become. In our story today God makes another unexpected choice.

Mary was a young woman, possibly as young as fourteen or fifteen. She was engaged to a carpenter named Joseph. She lived in a town called Nazareth in Galilee. She was not rich or well-known. She didn't even live in a important town. But one day something very important happened to her.

The angel Gabriel was sent by God to speak to Mary. He appeared to her and said, "Greetings, you who are highly favored! The Lord is with you." Mary must have been very surprised by this appearance. She did not understand why the angel would call her "favored." But the angel said to her, "Do not be afraid, Mary, for you have found favor with God. He has chosen you to have a very special baby. You will name him Jesus, and he will be the Son of the Most High." Mary still did not understand how this could happen. But the angel said, "Nothing is impossible with God."

Mary believed what the angel told her, and the angel went away. Mary hurried to the house of her relative, Elizabeth, to share the good news with her. Mary sang a song of praise to God (see box).

What Mary said was true. All these centuries later we recognize her as the mother of our Lord, chosen by God. She was not rich or famous or important in the eyes of the world, but God chose her to have the most important baby who has ever been born.

> ## Mary's Song of Praise
> My soul magnifies the Lord, and my spirit rejoices in God my Savior, for he has looked with favor on the lowliness of his servant. Surely, from now on all generations will call me blessed; for the Mighty One has done great things for me; holy is his name.
>
> (Luke 1:46-49)

To Talk About

Ask: God chose Mary to be the mother of Jesus. Who might you have chosen to be the mother of such an important baby? Someone rich? Someone wise? Someone important?

Say: Those things are not important to God, and that is not the kind of person God chose. Sometimes God makes unexpected choices. (*Talk with the girls about some unexpected choices they can think of: Joseph as a leader in Egypt; David as a slayer of giants; David as a king; four fisherman and Matthew the tax collector as apostles.*)

Activity Choices

1. Bring plain, unpopped popcorn. Pass the popcorn around and let each girl take some. Talk with them about the popcorn. What is it? Can you eat it? If you did not know what happens to popcorn when you cook it, would you think it was good to eat? What do you think the first person to discover popcorn felt? Did he or she know what to expect? We know that popcorn is good because we know the potential hidden inside the kernel. Talk about the word *potential*. What does it mean? Potential means something that can happen but has not yet happened. God also knows the potential hidden inside each of us. God sees not only what we are, but what we can become with God's help.

Pop the corn and enjoy it with the girls.

2. You will need unpopped popcorn (multicolored popcorn would add interest to the activity), glue, posterboard, an instant-developing camera, magnetic tape, and markers. You can also provide a variety of items such as glitter, sequins, ribbon, lace, and so forth.

Make posterboard frames by cutting a square of posterboard with an opening in the middle the appropriate size for an instant-developing photo.

Have each girl write "God Sees What I Can Become" on her frame.

Let the girls decorate their frames with popcorn and any other items you have provided.

Activity Supplies

1. plain, unpopped popcorn; popcorn popper
2. unpopped popcorn; glue; posterboard; instant-developing camera; magnetic tape; markers; items to decorate with

Take a picture of each girl and allow her to tape it to her frame. Add magnetic tape to the back of the frames so that they can be displayed on the refrigerator. A frame this heavy will need two large strips of tape to hold it up. (If you are unable to take pictures, the girls can simply decorate a small square or heart from posterboard with the caption and popcorn to create a magnet.)

Suggested Book

Amazing Grace by Mary Hoffman. Talk about how the people around Grace judged her from the outside and not from the inside. Stress that even though the book does not talk about it, the way we can accomplish great things is not by ourselves, but with God's help.

Write God's Word on Your Heart

Psalm 139:1. This verse is about how God knows us. God knows everything about us, so God also knows what we can become.

Daily Beauty Treatment

Luke 1:46-49

Spiritual Aerobics

Spend a few minutes talking about last week's spiritual aerobics. Did the girls keep up their "week of praise"? Be sure to encourage them in their spiritual exercises — tell them how you did too! For this week encourage the girls to begin each day thinking of some personal positive trait that is full of potential. This is a good week to mention privately to each girl some trait that you have observed.

Write God's Word on Your Heart
Psalm 139:1

Daily Beauty Treatment
Luke 1:46-49

Lesson 9 Mary Anoints Jesus
Worship

Scripture Reference
John 12:1-8;
(Luke 10:38-42;
John 11:1-44)

In Bethany there lived a man named Lazarus and his two sisters, Mary and Martha. They were friends of Jesus. When he was in Bethany, Jesus visited in their home. He had even raised Lazarus from the dead.

One day as Jesus was visiting in Bethany, Lazarus gave a dinner for him. During the dinner Mary took a pound of expensive perfume made from pure nard and anointed Jesus' feet and then wiped his feet with her hair. The whole house was filled with the fragrance of the perfume.

Some of the people at the dinner complained about what Mary had done. Judas, one of the disciples, the one who would later betray him, said, "Why was this perfume not sold so that the money could be given to the poor?" Jesus knew that Judas did not really care for the poor. He was in charge of the disciples' money, and he often helped himself to it.

Jesus defended Mary and what she had done. "Leave her alone," Jesus said. "She bought this perfume for the day of my burial. You will always have the poor with you, but you will not always have me." Jesus knew Mary was offering him a gift of love. The perfume she used to anoint him was very expensive, and she had offered it to Jesus. She had humbled herself before him, bowing down to anoint his feet and wipe them with her hair. Jesus knew the importance of what she had done for him in making this sacrifice.

To Talk About

Ask: Why did Mary anoint Jesus' feet with the expensive perfume? (*She was offering a gift of love to Jesus because of who he was and what he had done.*)

What can we offer to Jesus as a gift of love? (*We can offer ourselves to Jesus by doing the things he would want us to do. We can also give the gift of our worship.*)

What is worship? (*When we talk about worship, we usually think of the "worship services" we have at church. Find out what the girls think worship is. You might want to write some of the ideas they have on the board. They will probably list different things we do in worship, such as sing, pray, and so forth.*) So often we concentrate on what we do and not on why we do it. But singing, praying, and any other thing we do in worship are worthless if we do not know why we do them. (*Use the following questions and Scripture references to help the girls more fully understand worship.*)

Whom should we worship?

Why do we worship?

What does it mean to say that God or Jesus is holy?

Why did biblical people worship God or Jesus?

What things did they do when they worshiped?

Scripture references:

Exodus 20:1-6 (The commandments to worship only God. You may need to explain that Jesus and the Holy Spirit are God as well as God the Father.)

1 Chronicles 16:7-36 (David's song after the Ark of the Covenant was returned — includes thanksgiving, praise, affirmation of the holiness and power of God, and recounting of the things that God had done for God's people.)

2 Chronicles 6:1–7:10 (The dedication of the Temple by Solomon. Includes Solomon speaking to the people, prayer, praise, music, offerings, and celebration.)

Matthew 14:22-33 (After Jesus walks on water, those in the boat worship him in the realization that he is the Son of God.)

John 4:10-24 (Jesus, talking with the Samaritan woman about where to worship, says that it will not matter where you worship, but how — "in spirit and in truth."

John 12:1-11 (Today's story of Jesus being anointed by Mary. In the giving of this gift, she worships Jesus.)

1 Corinthians 10:14-17 (The Lord's Supper is a participation in the death of Jesus.)

Revelation 4:6-11 (An example of worship in heaven.)

Revelation 22:8-9 (John is told by the angel not to worship him, but to worship only God.)

Psalm 99:5 (Worship God, who is holy.)

Say: The Bible tells us that we are not to worship idols, other people, or even angels. We are to worship God, the Father, the Son, and the Holy Spirit. In the examples above, people worshiped God or Jesus because they realized the holiness of God. They also worshiped because they were thankful for the things that God or Jesus had done for them. They did not worship because they had to or because it was a rule. Their worship was a gift of love, just like the gift of perfume that Mary gave when she anointed Jesus. The worship that we see in the Bible is full of praise that the people offered to God or Jesus. Also, in many of the examples of worship in the Bible, the people bowed down on the ground to show respect and reverence.

Ask: What can we learn about worship from these Scriptures? (*We should worship for the same reasons that people in the Bible did—not because we have to, but because we want to. We should give our time of worship as a gift to God. We should give this gift to God out of love. In our worship we should praise God and thank God for the things God has done. We should remember those things as we worship. This is the reason that we take the Lord's Supper during worship. By doing this, we are remembering what Jesus did for us when he died.*)

Say: Worship is a celebration of God, but it should also be respectful. We should always remember that God is the creator of everything. God is more powerful than anything else. God made us and everything around us. We should remember that Jesus, God's only begotten Son, came to earth, lived, died, and rose again because he loves us.

Activity Choices

1. Bring net, tulle, or fabric printed with flowers; ribbon; silk flowers; and potpourri. Allow the girls to make a potpourri sachet for someone they love. Cut the fabric into circles about eight to ten inches in diameter. Show the girls how to put some of the potpourri in the center of the fabric and then gather the fabric together. Secure the top with a rubber band and tie a ribbon around it. Add silk flowers to the tie or glue them to the sachet using a cool-melt glue gun. As the girls work, talk about the gift that Mary gave to Jesus to show her love for him. Talk about the gifts we can give to Jesus and to others to show our love.

2. You will need small boxes with removable lids, wrapping paper, and gift bows. Allow the girls to cover the lids and boxes separately with wrapping paper and to add bows to the tops. On small pieces of paper let them write gifts that we can give to God. Place these in the boxes and encourage the girls to take them home and to look at them often.

Suggested Book

What Does God Do? by Hans Wilhelm. This beautiful book uses Scriptures from Job and the Psalms to explain the holiness of God. This would be an excellent book to use in introducing the concept of praise to your girls.

Write God's Word on Your Heart

Revelation 5:12

Daily Beauty Treatment

Revelation 5:6-14

Spiritual Aerobics

How have the girls been doing with their spiritual aerobics? How have you been doing? Are there any that you and/or the girls have kept up from week to week? This week encourage the girls to set a behavior goal related to worship. Perhaps they might choose to have a personal devotional time each day. Another option would be to share a devotional time with a family member or a friend at least once this week.

Activity Supplies
1. fabric printed with flowers, ribbon, silk flowers, and potpourri, scissors, rubber bands (optional: glue gun)
2. small boxes with removable lids, wrapping paper, and gift bows, tape, paper, pens or pencils

Write God's Word on Your Heart Revelation 5:12

Daily Beauty Treatment Revelation 5:6-14

Lesson 10 Lydia
Hospitality

Scripture Reference
Acts 16:11-15

Note: *Because the focus of this lesson is hospitality, consider having this session in your home or in the home of someone who lives near the church. This will exemplify the idea of hospitality for the girls.*

In the New Testament the Book of Acts tells us about the beginning and the spread of the church. Paul was one of the important persons involved in the spread of the church. Paul traveled to many places on missionary journeys to teach people about Jesus. On one of these journeys he traveled with a man named Silas. They went to the city of Philippi, a Roman city and the leading city of Macedonia. They stayed there for several days. Do you remember the book in the New Testament named Philippians? This is a letter that Paul wrote to the Christians in Philippi after he had left.

On the sabbath Paul and Silas went outside the city gate to the river. There was a place by the river where people met to pray on the sabbath. Paul and Silas found a group of women there worshiping and praying. Among the women was one named Lydia. Lydia was from the city of Thyatira. She sold purple cloth for a living. The city of Thyatira was famous for producing a special purple dye. This dye was very expensive, so the cloth that was made with this dye was very expensive. Only wealthy people and royalty could afford to buy it.

Lydia was a believer in God. She listened to the things that Paul and Silas taught about Jesus, and she believed them. Lydia and the members of her household were baptized. She asked Paul and Silas to stay in her home. Also, Lydia opened her home to the other Christians in Philippi so that they could meet there. Paul and Silas taught many people in Lydia's home. She was happy to welcome Paul and Silas into her home, as well as to provide a place for the Christians to meet.

To Talk About

Ask: Lydia showed hospitality. What does this word mean? In what ways did she show hospitality? What are some ways we can show hospitality?

Say: Christian hospitality includes not only having your friends over to your house, but also being willing to share the things that you have with others who are in need. This is more difficult.

Ask: What are ways that we can be hospitable to those in need?

Read: Romans 12:13; 1 Timothy 5:10; and 1 Peter 4:9. In two of these Scriptures Christians are told to practice hospitality. In the other, showing hospitality is found in a list of good deeds. Discuss the Scriptures with the girls.

Activity Choices

1. Provide materials for the girls to make a welcome banner for the foyer of the church or for the entry to the educational area. Suggested materials can include felt, fabric, glitter and paint pens. sequins, buttons, and so forth. If you have a small class, all the girls can work together on one banner. However, if your class is large, you will want to divide them into smaller groups, each making a separate banner. Encourage the girls to sketch their ideas on paper before they begin. Suggest that they keep the design simple and the caption short. As they work, make sure that labor is divided so that no one is left out of the process. It is sometimes helpful to assign specific jobs to each member of the group.

2. Obtain visitor cards from recent weeks from the church office. Provide blank cards and allow the girls to each write a note thanking one of the visitors for attending. Have the girls sign their names and "fourth, (fifth, sixth) grade class" to explain to the visitors that these letters were written by young people.

3. Prepare a hospitality grab bag. Before class gather items you would need if you were going to have a guest stay overnight in your home (clean towels, soft blankets and pillows, a special snack, a toothbrush, soap, alarm clock, and a fun game to play or a movie to watch). Put these items in a large bag or box. Invite each girl to draw an item from the bag and talk about how it would be used. When all the items are out of the bag, ask the girls if there are other things they can think of that they might have ready when a friend spends the night. Talk about the joy of having friends come to stay with us. Lydia showed hospitality to Paul and Silas when she asked them to stay in her home.

4. Bring items for the girls to make simple snacks (cherries and pineapple chunks, cheese cubes, celery, peanut butter, cookies, and so forth). Let the girls prepare a simple party by arranging the food on party trays. Invite another class to come in to share the snack with the girls.

Activity Supplies
1. felt, fabric, glitter and paint pens, sequins, buttons
2. blank visitor cards, pens or pencils

Activity Supplies
3. clean towels, soft blankets and pillows, a special snack, a toothbrush, soap, alarm clock, a fun game to play or a movie to watch, large bag or box

Write God's
Word on
Your Heart
Romans 12:13

Daily Beauty
Treatment
Matthew 25:31-46

Suggested Book

The Relatives Came by Cynthia Rylant. Read this book with the girls and talk about what the story teaches about hospitality. Some things you might mention are sharing food, overlooking inconveniences, making new memories, and so forth. Discuss times they have had people in their homes. What is their favorite part of having someone visit? What is difficult about having someone visit?

Write God's Word on Your Heart

Romans 12:13

Daily Beauty Treatment

Matthew 25:31-46

Spiritual Aerobics

The girls can set a behavior goal this week related to hospitality; for example, invite a new friend to your home. Encourage the girls to make some special preparations before the visit such as preparing a snack and planning activities.

Note: Next week's lesson is about Dorcas. Encourage the girls to look through their clothing for things they can no longer wear. (You might want to send a note home about this.) They can bring these items with them next week. Tell them to bring only items that are good and can be used—nothing that is worn out or torn up.

Note: One of the activity choices for next week is to decorate T-shirts for a younger class. Read through this activity. If you decide to do this activity, you will need to gather materials this week, especially if you plan to solicit donations.

Dorcas
Service

Scripture Reference
Acts 9:32-43

Note: *It is time to send out the letter to parents informing them about the closing ceremony and their part in this. Remember that this letter is not to be seen by the girls. It might be a good idea to make a simple invitation to the ceremony that the girls can take home with them next week as a reminder.*

In the town of Joppa, there lived a woman named Tabitha. This was her Aramaic name. She was also known as Dorcas, which is a Greek name. Dorcas was a Christian woman who spent much of her time helping the poor and those in need. She made clothing for widows and for others who did not have enough. All those in Joppa loved Dorcas because of her kindness.

One day Dorcas became ill and later died. The people who knew her were very sad. They washed her body and placed it in an upstairs room. Some of the Christians in Joppa heard that Peter was in Lydda, a town nearby. They sent two men to Peter and begged him to come quickly to Joppa.

When Peter arrived, he was taken to the upstairs room where they had laid Dorcas. The widows were crying and showing him clothing that Dorcas had made while she was alive. Peter sent them out of the room and got down on his knees. After saying a prayer, he turned to Dorcas and said, "Tabitha, get up." She opened her eyes and sat up. Peter helped her to her feet and called the others back into the room. They were excited and amazed by what had happened. They were glad to have Dorcas back with them.

To Talk About

Ask: Why did the people love Dorcas so much? Dorcas was a servant. In what ways can we be like Dorcas?

Discuss ways that your church family serves others as Dorcas did. In what ways can the girls become involved in some of these ministries?

The reading last week was about serving others. Talk about how Jesus said we serve him by serving others.

Activity Choices

1. Collect the clothing the girls have brought from home. Provide hangers and boxes so that the girls can hang and neatly fold the clothing to be organized and given away. If your church family has a clothing giveaway program, take the clothing to that area to be put away. If possible, have someone from that ministry talk to the girls and help them put the clothing in the right places. If your church does not have a clothing ministry, investigate what community programs are available for distributing clothing to needy families. Talk with the girls about what this program does. If possible, have a guest speaker who is involved with the work come and speak.

2. Dorcas was well-remembered for the things, especially clothing, that she made for others. Choose a class of younger children and allow the girls in your class to decorate T-shirts for the children in this class. You can purchase fabric paint or just use acrylic craft paint. You can also purchase fabric medium to add to the acrylic paint if you would like. White child-sized T-shirts are very inexpensive at discount or wholesale stores. If your budget does not cover this, ask individual church members if they would be willing to purchase one or two packages of three. The cost of a three-pack is around $4 or $5. To prepare the shirts for painting, stretch them over pieces of cardboard cut into a rectangle as illustrated below.

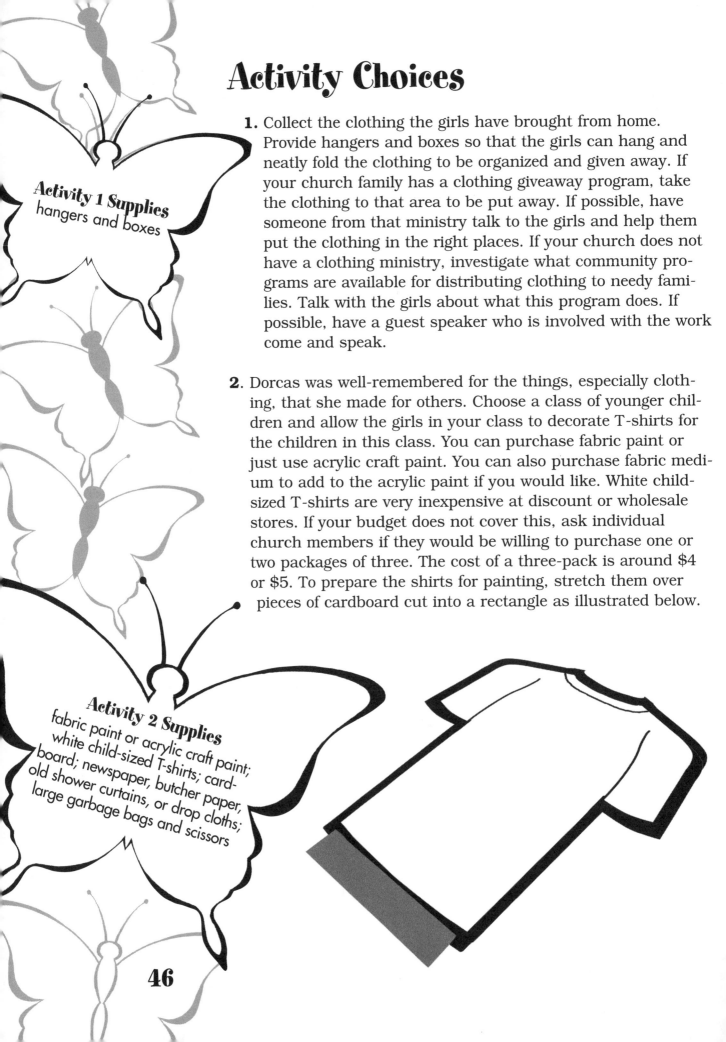

To get an approximate size, lay a T-shirt over the cardboard and trace around the body portion. The rectangle should be slightly larger than the shirt. Having the shirts stretched in this way provides a flat work surface and prevents paint from soaking through to the other side. Covering the cardboard with foil will prevent the shirts from sticking to the cardboard. If this preparation seems overwhelming to you, you might enlist the help of high school students or adults who might be unwilling to teach Bible classes but would be happy to help in this way.

Obviously, painting can be very messy, so be sure to cover your floor with newspaper, butcher paper, old shower curtains, or drop cloths. Provide paint smocks made of large garbage bags for the girls. (Cut armholes in the bottom corners and a neck hole between them.)

Some simple methods of shirt decoration are spatter paint, string paint, or sponge prints.

To spatter paint, you can use toothbrushes. Dip the toothbrushes in paint. Hold the toothbrush near the shirt and run a finger across the bristles, causing the paint to spatter onto the shirt. Another method of spatter painting is to use small paintbrushes. Dip the brushes in paint, and allow the excess paint to drip off. Then throw the paint off the end of the brush by flicking the wrist sharply.

String painting is a neater option. Provide several colors of paint and string cut into about 18-inch lengths. Allow the girls to dip the string into the paint and then lower onto the shirts. As the string is lowered onto the shirt, it will coil into interesting designs. Strings should be used for only one color, so provide several strings for each color of paint.

Sponges in a variety of shapes are available inexpensively from craft or discount stores. After the paint dries, you might want to add a simple caption such as "Celebrate God's Love" with fabric markers or slick paint.

The T-shirts will have to dry, so plan on giving them to the children on the following week. Check with the teacher of your younger class to make sure you have enough T-shirts for each child in the class.

Suggested Books

Magical Hands by Marjorie Barker and **Miss Tizzy** by Libba M. Gray. *Magical Hands* is a beautiful book about service among a group of friends. *Miss Tizzy* tells the story of an older woman who befriends neighborhood children. When she becomes ill, the children are given the opportunity to serve her.

Write God's Word on Your Heart

Matthew 20:26

Daily Beauty Treatment

Ephesians 2:5-10

Spiritual Aerobics

Have the girls set a goal related to service this week. Suggest that this not be one of their normal chores, but something special that they will do for this week.

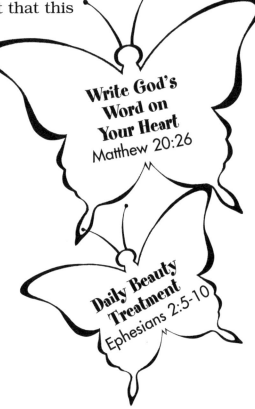

Write God's Word on Your Heart
Matthew 20:26

Daily Beauty Treatment
Ephesians 2:5-10

Priscilla
Teaching and Kindness

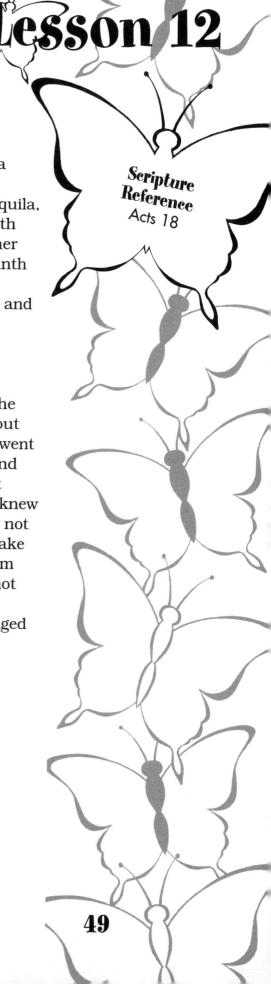

Scripture Reference
Acts 18

As Paul traveled on his missionary journeys, he met a couple in Corinth who were Christians. Their names were Aquila and Priscilla. Priscilla worked with her husband, Aquila, as a tentmaker. Paul was also a tentmaker and worked with them while he was in Corinth. Priscilla also worked with her husband teaching others about Jesus. Paul stayed in Corinth for quite a while, but eventually he went on to Ephesus to teach the people there. Aquila and Priscilla went with him and continued to work with him in teaching there. Paul left Ephesus, but Aquila and Priscilla stayed.

While they were there, a man named Apollos came to Ephesus. Apollos was a Jew who had been taught about the way of the Lord. He was a very good speaker and went about teaching others what he had learned. Priscilla and Aquila went to hear Apollos preach. They were pleased at how boldly and well he spoke, but they found that he had not been taught about the baptism of Jesus. When they learned this, they knew that he needed to be taught more completely, but they did not want to do anything to embarrass Apollos. They did not make fun of him or publicly put him down. Instead, they took him aside lovingly and talked to him about the things he had not learned. Later, Apollos wanted to continue his teaching in other places, and the Christians there in Ephesus encouraged him to do this.

To Talk About

Say: Priscilla helped her husband in teaching people about Jesus.

Priscilla and Aquila taught in a loving way, not in a way that embarrassed or made fun of people.

Priscilla and Aquila gave of their time to teach others about Jesus. They even moved with Paul to teach others.

In what ways can the girls take part in teaching others about Jesus? One very important way that people teach is through example. Talk about what an example is. How can the girls be a good example for others? Who might be seeing them and learning from their example? (*younger children, friends at school*)

Activity Choices

1. Read together Ephesians 4:15.

Say: This Scripture talks about speaking the truth in love. This is what Priscilla and Aquila did. They were very loving in the way that they taught Apollos. Sometimes people are not loving when they teach others. They make fun of what the other people believe. They may act as if they are better than others. This is not a loving way to teach.

Give each girl a sheet of paper. On one side, allow them to draw a heart. On the other side, allow them to draw a frowny face. Discuss and let the girls write down loving and nonloving ways to teach people on the appropriate sides of the paper. It would be fun to allow them to roleplay some of these examples of good and bad teachers. Let them keep the papers in their folders.

Activity Supplies
1. Bibles, paper, pens or pencils
2. paper, pens or pencils

2. Talk with the girls about being an example. People learn what we believe not only by what we say, but also by what we do. Give each girl a sheet of paper. Have each girl write on one side of the paper the names of at least two specific people to whom they can be an example. On the other side of the paper, have them write down at least two ways in which each girl can be an example.

3. Next week is the closing ceremony for *Beautiful in God's Eyes*. Allow the girls to create invitations for the special people they want to attend the ceremony.

Write God's Word on Your Heart

Ephesians 4:15

Daily Beauty Treatment

1 Timothy 4:6-16

Spiritual Aerobics

You might have the girls think of a specific way in which they can be examples during the week

Write God's
Word on
Your Heart
Ephesians 4:15

Suggested Book

Wild Lies and Secret Truth by Matt Tullos. One of the books in the Summit High Series, this book will help girls in the 12- to 14-year-old age range recognize the difference between truth and lies. For younger girls, choose **Enid and the Church Fire** by Cynthia G. Williams. Enid and her friends try to understand why someone would set their neighborhood church on fire, and they learn an important lesson about forgiveness.

Daily Beauty
Treatment
1 Timothy 4:6-16

Lesson 13 Closing Ceremony

The closing ceremony for this class can be patterned after a graduation ceremony. Set up the room with chairs at the front for each of the participants and chairs for the visitors. Prepare certificates for each of the girls as well as a small gift for you to give them.

A Possible Agenda for the Ceremony

Welcome and explanation of the class.

Reading of 1 Samuel 16:7 and Proverbs 31:30. (You might ask two of the girls to do these readings.)

Personal comment honoring an accomplishment, growth you have observed, or other characteristic of each girl.

Presentation of certificates and personal comment honoring an accomplishment, growth you have observed, or other characteristic of each girl.

Presentation of gifts and letters of blessing from family members.

General blessing for the girls.

Special music.

Special prayer.

Invite guests to share in reception.

Some Ways to Make the Event Special

1. Have each girl come forward individually. Present her certificate and make a personal comment to her about some growth, accomplishment, or characteristic you have observed in her through the course of the class.

2. Prepare a reception with all the trimmings. Bring out the best tablecloth, punch bowl, and special refreshments. Encourage the girls to dress up in their Sunday best and you do the same. (Be sensitive, however, if there are girls in the class who do not have "Sunday clothes." If this is the case, it would be better for the girls to wear their T-shirts.)

3. Invite a few of the talented singers from your congregation to prepare and to present a special song. This could be a special hymn or another appropriate song.

Special Blessing

I thank God for the chance to work with you in this class. Each of you is special and important to me and to God. It is my prayer that you will grow in faith with God each day. I pray that you will follow God and look for God's will for you. May you grow more beautiful in God's eyes every day.

Event 2 Supplies
tablecloth, punch bowl, and special refreshments

Charts and Patterns

1. Attendance Chart

2. Bible Chart

3. Memory Work Chart

4. Take-Home Memory Work Reminders

5. Prayer Partner Reminder pattern

6. Letterhead

7. Daily Bible Reading Chart

8. Personal Spiritual Discipline Plan

9. Butterfly Pattern for T-shirts

10. Closing Ceremony Invitation

    Completion Certificate

Becoming Beautiful in God's eyes

Name_____

Let God's word change your life.

Write God's Word on Your Heart

Name _____

Proverbs 31:30

Ephesians 5:21

Hebrews 13:6

Matthew 23:11-12

Ruth 1:16

1 Samuel 1:27

Philippians 4:4

Psalm 139:1

Revelation 5:12

Romans 12:13

Matthew 20:26

Ephesians 4:15

Write God's Word on your heart.

"Pray in the Spirit at all times in every prayer and supplication."

Ephesians 6:18

Name:_____

"Pray in the Spirit at all times in every prayer and supplication."

Ephesians 6:18

Name:_____

Beautiful in God's Eyes

For the LORD does not see as mortals see; they look on the outward appearance, but the LORD looks on the heart.

1 Samuel 16:7b

Daily Beauty Treatment

Scripture_____

Date_____

Name_____

Sunday_____

Monday_____

Tuesday_____

Wednesday_____

Thursday_____

Friday_____

Saturday_____

61

Spiritual Aerobics Training Plan

Name _____

Week 1

Week 2

Week 3

Week 4

Week 5

Week 6

Week 7

Week 8

Week 9

Week 10

Week 11

Week 12

Use to make a T-shirt transfer

Beautiful
in God's Eyes

You're invited to a very special ceremony honoring

_____

and the other girls who have been taking part in the course

"Beautiful in God's Eyes."

Please come share in this special time with us.

Date _____

Time _____

Location _____

CERTIFICATE OF COMPLETION

_____

has completed the course

"Beautiful in God's Eyes"

We pray that she will strive to grow more
beautiful in God's eyes each day.

Date_____   Teacher_____

Location_____

*"For the LORD does not see as mortals see; they look on the outward appearance,
but the LORD looks on the heart."*

1 Samuel 16:7b